Last Tango

A play

Mike Harding

Samuel French - London
New York - Toronto - Hollywood

© 1992 BY MOONRAKER PRODUCTIONS LTD.

Rights of Performance by Amateurs are controlled by Samuel French Ltd, 52 Fitzroy Street, London W1P 6JR, and they, or their authorized agents, issue licences to amateurs on payment of a fee. **It is an infringement of the Copyright to give any performance or public reading of the play before the fee has been paid and the licence issued.**

The Royalty Fee indicated below is subject to contract and subject to variation at the sole discretion of Samuel French Ltd.

> Basic fee for each and every
> performance by amateurs   Code M
> in the British Isles

The Professional Rights in this play are controlled by CASAROTTO RAMSAY LTD, 60 WARDOUR STREET, LONDON W1V 3HP.

The publication of this play does not imply that it is necessarily available for performance by amateurs or professionals, either in the British Isles or Overseas. Amateurs and professionals considering a production are strongly advised in their own interests to apply to the appropriate agents for consent before starting rehearsals or booking a theatre or hall.

ISBN 0 573 01822 7

Please see page iv for further copyright information.

LAST TANGO IN WHITBY

First produced at the Nottingham Playhouse on 5th April 1990, with the following cast of characters:

Kathleen	Paula Tilbrook
Jimmy	James Tomlinson
Joan	Ann Aris
Henry	Cliff Howells
Maureen/Mrs Mingham	Maureen O'Reilly
Pat	Judith Barker
Jessie	Margo Stanley
Phil	Freddie Lees
Edna	Janet Whiteside
Driver/Honeymooner/Waiter/ Jet Shop Man/Gino/John	Jeffrey Longmore
Edie/Clare/Waitress/Sally	Sarah Henderson Harding
Alice/Honeymooner/Debbie	Susie McKenna

Directed by Kenneth Alan Taylor
Designed by Karen Bartlett
Choreography by Judith Barker

COPYRIGHT INFORMATION

(See also page ii)

This play is fully protected under the Copyright Laws of the British Commonwealth of Nations, the United States of America and all countries of the Berne and Universal Copyright Conventions.

All rights, including Stage, Motion Picture, Radio, Television, Public Reading, and Translation into Foreign Languages, are strictly reserved.

No part of this publication may lawfully be reproduced in ANY form or by any means—photocopying, typescript, recording (including video-recording), manuscript, electronic, mechanical, or otherwise—or be transmitted or stored in a retrieval system, without prior permission.

Licences for amateur performances are issued subject to the understanding that it shall be made clear in all advertising matter that the audience will witness an amateur performance; that the names of the authors of the plays shall be included on all announcements and on all programmes; and that the integrity of the authors' work will be preserved.

The Royalty Fee is subject to contract and subject to variation at the sole discretion of Samuel French Ltd.

In Theatres or Halls seating Four Hundred or more the fee will be subject to negotiation.

In Territories Overseas the fee quoted in this Acting Edition may not apply. A fee will be quoted on application to our local authorized agent, or if there is no such agent, on application to Samuel French Ltd, London.

VIDEO RECORDING OF AMATEUR PRODUCTIONS

Please note that the copyright laws governing video-recording are extremely complex and that it should not be assumed that any play may be video-recorded *for whatever purpose* without first obtaining the permission of the appropriate agents. The fact that a play is published by Samuel French Ltd does not indicate that video rights are available or that Samuel French Ltd controls such rights.

CHARACTERS

Jimmy
Henry
Kathleen
Joan
Maureen
Jessie
Pat
Alice }
Edie } non-speaking
Driver
Phil
Edna
Jet Shop Man
Young Man }
Young Woman } honeymooners, non-speaking
Clare
Debbie
Mrs Mingham
Gino
Tea Girls
Sally
John

The action of the play takes place in and around Whitby
Time: the present

SYNOPSIS OF SCENES

ACT I   SCENE 1   The coach
        SCENE 2   The hotel foyer
        SCENE 3   The amusement arcade
        SCENE 4   The jet shop
        SCENE 5   The Abbey
        SCENE 6   The hotel dining-room
        SCENE 7   The ballroom
        SCENE 8   The beach
        SCENE 9   The ballroom
        SCENE 10 The pier

ACT II SCENE 1   The ballroom
        SCENE 2   The beach
        SCENE 3   The ballroom
        SCENE 4   The tearoom
        SCENE 5   A shelter on the prom
        SCENE 6   The foyer
        SCENE 7   The foyer/The ballroom/The bus station

A licence issued by Samuel French Ltd to perform this play does NOT include permission to use any Incidental music specified in this copy. Where the place of performance is already licensed by the Performing Right Society a return of the music used must be made to them. If the place of performance is not so licensed then application should be made to the PERFORMING RIGHT SOCIETY, 29 Berners Street, London W1.

A separate and additional licence from PHONOGRAPHIC PERFORMANCES LTD, Ganton House, Ganton Street, London W1, is needed whenever commercial recordings are used.

ACT I

Scene 1

The coach

Music—"Last Tango" or Cliff Richard's "Summer Holiday" or a suitable tango tune

There are two rows of seats on trolleys facing the audience, severely raked

The couples dance on together. Pat and Jessie dance on with their suitcases. To overcome a clumsy opening curtain the actors could board the coach with bits of business, dancing on stage, pushing their cases under the trolleys, building the opening as the music plays

Henry sits by the Driver, Kathleen, Maureen and Jessie behind Henry, Joan and Jimmy on the other side of the aisle. Pat sits alone, well behind the others. A sense of travel could be achieved using sound effects and back projection. The actors once settled sing a medley of "Una Paloma Blanca"

As the different pieces of action take place, lighting changes focus our attention on the actors

Jimmy, with a party hat on, walks up and down the coach giving out bottles of light ale and Guinness

Jimmy Now Henry, what fettle?
Henry Good fettle, Jim.
Kathleen Tell that driver to slow down, he must be on piece work. He very near had us over on the last bend. Drivin' like Niki bloomin' Lauda.
Henry Some speed, eh?
Jimmy Who's peed?
Joan I don't know about the others but I have.

Laughter

Henry Come on Jim, me throat thinks me belly's cut.
Jimmy All right, wait your bloody sweat.
Joan What about the girls? This is the age of liberation you know, what's Guinness for the goose is Guinness for the gander.
Jimmy Some holiday this is going to be, I'm like a frigging waiter here! Up and down like a bride's nightie!
Maureen Hey come on. Who voted himself in charge of the ale?
Henry Jimmy did.
Kathleen Exactly the same as last year.
Jessie And the year before.

Jimmy Alice, Edie. Do you want one, Edie? Alice, can I give you one?
Joan Best offer you'll have today.
Jimmy Eh I'm behind at home as it is.

He gets the bottles and hands them out as the coach sways along and the trippers sing "Oh Oh Antonio"

Henry knows every inch of the road and is making sure the Driver gets the benefit of his wisdom

Henry Now then, young man. There's a straight bit coming up now, then there's a junction, well, not a junction, more a sort of a fork really, it's our right of way anyroad, then it's a bit of a steep hill with a kink in it like a bit of a dog's leg, then a narrow bridge.
Driver (*polite, but bored already*) Oh ay.
Henry Ay and watch the bridge. August Bank Holiday nineteen fifty-three there were two charabancs locked solid, side by side on that bridge. Traffic were jammed for four hours. They had to get two tanks from Catterick Camp to pull 'em apart. Traffic went all the way back to Malton.
Driver You don't say.
Henry Ay, you can still see the scratches on the bridge, if you look.
Driver Very interestin' that.
Henry I know this road like the back of me 'and. I were a dispatch rider durin' t'war and I were always up and down here, carryin' messages. That were before I were sent abroad. North Africa it were. We weren't bothered about Rommel. It was the dysentery that got you. I've seen latrines that were just planks over a ten-foot trench, lined up for miles — and thousands of squaddies in a line crappin' their insides out. Watch this lane on the left, a farmer come out of there in a hay wagon in forty-nine — took a coach driver's head off. Scorpions were bad an' all. My mate got bit by a scorpion. Fellow sergeant.
Driver What, the scorpion?
Henry I never got dysentery you know — all through North Africa — never had it . . .
Driver No?
Henry Dosed mesen wi' Andrews Liver Salts, mornin' noon and night. Blasted the little buggers out. I could eat plates of greasy compo and all that Arab food while me best mate had an arse like a ripped wellie. Just watch it, there's an overhanging tree comin' up round the next bend.

Pause

Well bugger me! They must have cut it down!
Driver (*laconically*) Maybe it 'ad dysentery.
Henry (*seriously*) Trees don't get dysentery you pillock! (*Turning behind him to the others, he taps the side of his head and winks*)
Driver (*under his breath*) Oh Jesus why me? Why me!
Kathleen So I said — "I don't care if it does have to come from the other side of the world, young man, I don't care if it's got to come from Mars. I'm not paying seventy-five pence——"

Act I, Scene 1

Jessie Seventy-five pence?
Kathleen "—seventy-five pence for a tin of corned beef," I said. It was that cheeky one with the moustache and the patent-leather hair, you know, the one whose uncle was had up for exposing himself on the bandstand in Jubilee Park.
Jessie Jubilee Park.
Kathleen Seventy-five pence!
Jessie Jubilee Park.

They all look at her

Maureen They'll rob you blind given half a chance. They'll steal your eye and come back for the socket!
Kathleen "That's fifteen shillings in old money," I said. For a small tin of corned beef.
Jessie (*open-mouthed*) Small tin!
Maureen I don't know how they get away with it, it's only seventy-two at the corner shop and that's supposed to be dearer than the Co-op.
Kathleen And you could still see the old price sticker for seventy-one pence underneath.
Jessie Underneath.
Kathleen I said it's funny how it's suddenly gone up four pence overnight.
Jessie Overnight!
Maureen Did you buy it?
Kathleen (*frostily*) Indeed I did not. I made him slice me some brawn and I had that instead, with a bit of piccalilli and a boiled egg. I had heartburn something terrible afterwards. Used up a full packet of Rennies and the corner shop was shut.
Jessie (*thinking*) You could have gone to "open all hours"—Mr Patel's.
Maureen Ooh! You know I wouldn't buy my stuff there on principle. You never know where it's been.
Jessie You can't do much to a packet of Rennies.
Kathleen (*knowingly, and thus declaring an end to the debate*) That's what you think. They have ways and means they do. The ones next to our Florence's slaughtered a goat over a grid in the back yard while she got her washing out. Her best loose covers could have been ruined.
Jessie But there's a great big wall between them.
Kathleen That's not the point. A bit more wind and she could have had goat's blood all over her dralon. Your trouble is you're too trusting you are, Jessie. You let folk take you for granted, you do.
Jimmy (*reaching Maureen, Jessie and Kathleen*) All right girls?
Maureen Yes thanks, Jimmy.
Jimmy Another Guinness?
Jessie Oh no, thank you, Jimmy, we've not finished this one yet.
Jimmy You've had that since Wakefield, get it supped up.
Kathleen Yes well, some of us aren't going to spend the next week on our backs.
Joan You speak for yourself! I've brought a new nightie and four gallons of Paco Rabane perfume! I hope your heart's all right Jim, 'cos it's oysters and brown ale as soon as we get off this chara.

Jimmy Joan read this article in the *Cosmopolitan*. It says at our age we ought to try out some new positions like, you know this *soixante-neuf*. We're going to give it a try or, failing that, two thirty and a halfs or a thirty-six with crispy noodles and a thirty-three with chow mein and chips.

Jessie (*in a loud whisper to Kathleen*) What's he talking about?

Kathleen He's talking about what you can't eat again.

Maureen (*looking at Henry*) Men! It's all they ever think of.

Kathleen One-track minds.

Jessie What's numbers got to do with it?

Jimmy *Soixante-neuf* is sixty-nine.

Jessie You're not that old. You started at Inkerman Street School the year before me, you're only sixty-three.

Kathleen (*raising her eyes to heaven*) When ignorance is bliss.

Jimmy (*losing ground but still trying to get his message across*) It's a joke, Jessie, *soixante-neuf*, it's French numbers.

Henry (*shouting*) Better than French letters!!

General laughter. Kathleen looks stormily out of the window at the passing countryside. Maureen glares at him. Jessie still doesn't understand

Jessie I didn't know you knew anybody in France to write to, Jimmy.

Jimmy reacts. He whispers to the Driver. The coach stops

Jimmy Right lads, all out.

Kathleen Why are we stopping? This isn't a regulation stop.

Jimmy No, it's an emergency stop.

Jimmy, the Driver and Henry get out of the coach. All the women look out of the left side of the coach. Jessie squeals

Kathleen Avert your eyes, Jessie.

The men get back in the coach

Joan Eh Jimmy, I weren't half proud of ours.

Jimmy It's a littl'en but a minian.

Driver Right-oh, off we go again.

Jimmy (*starting to sing*) "We're off in a motor car..."

Pat comes up from the back

Pat Come on Jimmy, give us a Guinness.

Jimmy (*concerned*) Are you all right, Pat?

Pat Ay. I've had a bit of a weep but I'm all right now. Just feeling a bit sorry for myself.

Jimmy You do right. Get a drink—enjoy yourself. Arthur would want you to enjoy yourself.

Pat Ay he would, he would that, would Arthur. Bye, we've had some times together, haven't we, Jim?

They are holding on to the back of the seats, standing in the aisle throughout this next conversation

Act I, Scene 1

Jimmy We have that. He was a fair member was Arthur.
Pat He lived life, didn't he?
Jimmy Right to the last drop. Always laughing wasn't he? You hardly ever saw him without a smile on his face.
Pat He never missed one of these dos, did he? This would have been the thirteenth year if he'd lived.
Jimmy He'd have wanted you to come.
Pat Oh I know. He were never one to put himself first. You remember last year when his legs gave up we took him to the Polish Club in that wheelchair we borrowed from the health centre. "Get up and dance", he said, "never mind me, I've got a pint and some fags, I'm all right." And I did an' all, we had a good night.
Jimmy I remember, I had a dance with you.
Pat And every time I looked across he smiled and waved. And he meant it. He only stopped going out in the end because he was in too much pain and he thought he was too much trouble.
Jessie Too much trouble.
Joan (*coming up, a bit perturbed*) You all right love?
Pat (*shaking herself out of it*) Yes, just a bit sorry for meself that's all.
Jimmy Arthur wouldn't have had it, what would he have said?
Jimmy ⎫ (*together*) ⎧ "Nay gi'o'er—you're a long time dead, get supped up,
Pat ⎭ ⎩ give us a smile and gerrum in."

They laugh together

Jessie Gerrum in.
Jimmy Anyway, a bottle of Guinness for my favourite girl, after Joan that is. (*He kisses her*)
Henry Look at him, at it already! That bromide they put in the Naafi tea never did work!
Joan Leave him alone, it takes a bit of the pressure off me. He gets worse the older he gets.
Jimmy (*laughing, pulling out three fezzes from a carrier bag*) Look what I brought! I thought I might as well. We could 'ave a go.
Joan (*perturbed for a moment*) Jimmy?
Jimmy Well, we've got no Arthur but we've got Pat.

He sticks a fez on each of the two girls and on himself then starts the Wilson, Betty and Kepple sand dance—"Oompa Oompa" etc. They do a little of the sand dance in the aisle, then sit down to applause. The Driver turns to Henry

Driver Bloody geriatric delinquents—worse than football specials. Do you know, on one of these Golden Age Trips I did, there were a couple having it off on the back seat! Sixty-five years old, the pair of them going at it, hell for leather they were. On the back seat!
Henry Well, t'back seat's the only place you can stretch out!

Pause

(*Still talking at the Driver*) Now just over the next hill there's a cottage. Small thing it is, just a couple of rooms up and down. Well in nineteen forty-nine we were comin' over here in an old Leyland. Red it were, that hot Whitsun we 'ad. You're too young to remember. And anyroad it boiled over so the driver stopped at that cottage for some water. The woman come out, little bandy woman she was, wi' a bonnet on. She gi' us a bucket of water and the driver asked was there owt' ee could do for 'er. "Well, yes," she said. "Could you give me a little bit of petrol only I've got some grease spots on me coat and I want to clean them off." So he siphoned some petrol off, an old Foden it was, a one-two-seven crash gearbox—you know the one. Anyroad off we goes. A week later we're goin' back off us 'olidays and the old woman, she must 'ave bin waitin' for our coach 'cos she flagged us down. Seems like she's 'ad an accident wi' the petrol. She's put some in a saucer to dab on the coat and forgot it were there and put some milk in it for the cat. When t'cat come in it supped the milk and petrol and never noticed. T'owd lass were sat before t'fire an' the next thing were t'cat had run across t'room, climbed t'wall, run along one of t'beams, down t'wall on the other side, ran round the room a couple of dozen times screechin' its 'ead off. Well th'owd lass were terrified. Next thing is t'cat runs up t'curtains, springs off backwards and lands on the hearthrug, runs round the rug a couple of dozen times then all of a sudden stops and rolls over on its back wi' its legs in the air.

Driver Was it dead?

Henry Nay, were it 'ell as like. It'd run out of petrol. (*Laughing fit to die*) It'd run out of petrol! It'd run out of petrol! (*Rubbing his eyes*)

Driver (*not amused*) You dozy old bugger!

Henry It never fails to gerrum that one. Every driver we've had I've got wi' that 'un!

Pause

We're here.

The Driver looks sideways at him. They jerk forward as the coach "arrives"

Music—"Hernando's Hideaway"

The actors, singing "Hernando's Hideaway" dance off the coach and into . . .

SCENE 2

The terrace and foyer of the Royal Hotel

The Driver, Jimmy and Henry start to unload the cases

Phil and Edna enter, dressed in smart blazers and flannel skirt and trousers. Phil is wearing a cravat and they both wear straw boaters. They are roughly the same age as the people on the coach but dress younger and carry themselves in a way that belies their years. Phil is obviously quite happy to see the crowd, and immediately starts to help with the cases, Edna, on the other hand, has a fixed, sewn-on smile

Act I, Scene 2   7

The song ends on "Olé!"

Phil (*to them all generally*) Hallo there! Welcome to the Hotel Whitby. Have a good trip?
Jimmy Ay, it was all right.
Henry We nearly ran out of ale, the driver were too slow an' 'ee didn't know the road. Apart from that it were all right.
Phil I'm Phil and this is Edna. We're "The Shangri-Las", we'll be running the entertainments for the next week.

General "hallos"

Yes well, very nice.
Kathleen I hope you don't play any of that rock and roll or punk disco stuff. The couple we had last year were too modern for my liking—had two that I know of under the osteopath for six months. She, (*indicating Jessie*) went to bed every night with a crippling migraine.
Jessie Crippling migraine.
Phil (*laughing*) No, it's strictly old-time and progressive with a bit of fun thrown in.
Pat (*coming up with her suitcase*) We like a bit of fun us lot. What sort of fun?
Phil Anything you want within reason.
Pat Ey Jessie that leaves us plenty of scope then dun't it? We could 'ave a right rave up me and you. So what have you got for us then love?
Edna \} (*sourly with her fixed smile*) There'll be interval bingo, a raffle for a
Phil / giant teddy bear, a fancy dress competition, ballroom dances, spot prizes and a talent competition.
Pat Will there be any talent though? That's what we're lookin' for isn't it Jessie? A bit of talent. Summat young and full of fire. A toy boy about thirty-five with plenty of brass and a nice bum.
Jessie A nice bum. (*Realizing what she's said*) Ooh Pat.
Pat Well it'll do you good. It's better than Horlicks for makin' you sleep, you know.
Jessie Isn't she terrible?
Pat Given half the chance I am.
Phil (*laughing*) Well we'll 'ave to see what we can do. I'm not sure about a toy boy though. We'll keep our eyes out for you.
Pat (*smiling at him*) We'll keep you to that, won't we Jessie.
Jessie Yes we will. (*Pause*) What are you talking about, Pat?
Pat Nothing love, it doesn't matter.
Jimmy (*coming up with the last of the cases; to the crowd*) Right, same routine as usual. Check in, sling your bags, then down the *Star* for a pint of Cameron's, up the *Elsinor* for a couple more, then back for tea, right?

Music—Mississippi dip—Swanee

General yeses and OKs and they dance off on the trip round the town

Scene 3

Through a series of "snapshots", we see various couples walking through the September afternoon, the light is golden and warm. Music drives them on as they tango from scene to scene, laughing, going on space invaders, fruit machines, sitting at bingo in the Amusement Arcade. The caller calls out "Hairs in your teeth—69" and Jimmy shouts "House" and wins a big dayglo panda

Music—"The Gay Gordons"

Overall there is the sound of seagulls and the sense of a fish and chips seaside town. Maureen, Pat, Kathleen and Jessie, who've been seen as a group of women where the others are couples, are seen trying out a lucky dip machine. Jessie wins a key-ring with a spanner in it

Jessie Ooh, it's a key-ring with a little spanner in it.
Maureen It'll do for fixing your loose nuts.

Pat has a go and gets out a box; she opens it, there is a ring inside

Jessie Oh look, it's a wedding ring.

There is an awkward silence. Pat tries the cheap ring on and it fits

Pat Well maybe it'll bring me luck, you never know.
Jessie If Arthur was here he would have been booking for fishing by now.

Kathleen tries to shut her up. Pat sees the move

Pat It's all right. She's right. I don't feel bad about him. If Arthur was here he would have been down the *Star* having a few pints with Jimmy, booking a fishing trip with that fisherman with the nose full of boils.
Jessie Boils.
Pat But Arthur isn't here—he's dead.
Jessie He's dead.
Pat I am here and I'm not—and I'll tell you what Arthur would have wanted me to do—exactly what I'm going to do, have a bloody good time. Come on.

Music—Military Two-step

They dance round to . . .

Scene 4

The jet shop

Jet Shop Man Very popular in Victorian times were these. These are all Victorian pieces. They were very popular indeed, particularly with widows.

Pat puts the piece down, looking at him as though she thinks he is taking the mickey, then realizing he isn't and that the others have gone silent round her.

Act I, Scene 6

She turns to another tray and picks up a bright art deco badge shaped like an ice cream cone

Pat I'll have that one.
Jet Shop Man Are you not having the jet then?
Pat No, I want something a bit more cheerful.
Jet Shop Man Ay, well I must say I prefer the bright colours meself.
Pat Don't wrap it, I'll pin it on now. (*She does*)

They dance on to . . .

Music—Military Two-step

SCENE 5

The Abbey

Back projection to suggest the Abbey. A young couple are kissing and canoodling on the bench

Pat I love Whitby. I think of all the places I've been, this is my favourite town of them all. I love the Abbey.
Maureen You'd think they'd fix it up, wouldn't you?
Kathleen This is where Dracula came ashore, you know.
Jessie Dracula?
Maureen Yes, the vampire, you know. Like Henry, only with his own teeth.
Jessie I've never heard that before.
Kathleen I know, I read it in a book last year. He's supposed to have sailed here looking for a woman.
Jessie You'd think he'd be able to find a woman in his own country wouldn't you? Maybe he wanted someone foreign.

Pat nods towards the young couple on the bench. The boy's kissing the girl's neck; she, eyes closed, is obviously enjoying it

Pat Look, there he is over there.
Jessie (*squealing*) Where? (*She looks*) Oh, you didn't half give me a turn!
Kathleen It's disgusting, it shouldn't be allowed in public.
Maureen He looks as though he's eating her.
Pat Well he's probably still got his own teeth. Come on, it's making me hungry watching 'em.

Music—Military Two-step

They dance off, as the two waitresses dance on, pushing the table before them

SCENE 6

The hotel dining-room. The same evening

Plates are clattering. Two girls are cleaning up after dinner. In their late teens, they aren't intentionally cruel, but heartless in the way the young can sometimes be. They provide a great contrast to the older group

Clare So go on, what did he say to you then? This new boyfriend of yours.
Debbie He said he'd just been talkin' to her. I said, talkin' to her! With your hands on her tits and your tongue that far down her throat it's a wonder it weren't comin' out of 'er arse.
Clare You didn't say that did you?
Debbie Damn right I did. I'm not havin' 'im make a fool of me like that in front of all me mates. I walked off then and just left 'im stood there. Then me and Sarita went off to Henry Africa's and we got smashed and copped off. The last I saw of Sarita she were leanin' out of the window of a Cortina wavin' her knickers at me. It had a sticker on the back "Young Farmers do it in the mud". (*Pause*) The trouble is, Clare, I really love 'im. I'd give anythin' to get back wi' 'im.
Clare Lads mek me sick they do. They're so big-headed. Just for once I'd like to meet one that didn't come up and ask you where you worked when all the time he's just wondering how long it'll tek 'im ter get yer knickers down.

Pause

Debbie Have you done them menus?
Clare Yeah.
Debbie God, they eat like horses. They are supposed to be old and past it. You'd think this lot was eating up for the Olympics.
Clare What do they come here for anyway? The season's over in't it?
Debbie Have you never seen them before?
Clare No, what do they do?
Debbie Weren't you here last year?
Clare No, I started just before last Christmas.
Debbie Ay, I forgot. Well this lot's on a Heritage week.
Clare What's that when it's at home?
Debbie Well, we call it a "tango and touch up" week. It's a cheap holiday run by the Heritage travel company. They specialize in these off-season holidays for OAPs. Monday to Sunday inclusive for ninety-five quid.
Clare That's cheap.
Debbie Well it's out of season and if it wasn't for them this place'd be like a morgue. Come to think of it, it is like a morgue. Anyway, because everything's all-in including the entertainment, they don't have to spend anything. Some of them have been coming here for years.
Clare Who are those two with the blazers then?
Debbie The entertainers? "The Shangri-Las".
Clare "The Shangri-Las". Sounds like a gang of Japanese wrestlers.
Debbie You wait till you see them dancing, it's all that old-fashioned stuff. You know, the valletta, the tango, the foxtrot and that.

She grabs Clare and they begin dancing cheek-to-cheek between the tables

We then see the head waitress standing at the bottom of the room framed in white tables

Act I, Scene 7

Mrs Mingham Deborah! Clare! When you've both quite finished!
Debbie Sorry Mrs Mingham.
Clare She was just showin' me the valletta.
Mrs Mingham Well she'd better show you how to get this place cleaned up and laid for breakfast for a hundred and ten or I'll show you two the Job Centre Quickstep!
Debbie Yes, Mrs Mingham.
Clare Yes, Mrs Mingham.
Debbie That's what bein' married twenty-five years does to you. You'd never think she were like us once would you?
Clare What do you mean? Young and cynical! Instead of old and cynical?

They both laugh and dance off, pushing the table before them

Music—"Maybe It's Because I'm A Londoner"

Scene 7

The ballroom

The Lights focus on the mirror ball and then on the couples, who walk on and stand waiting in formation for the tango. Ladies stand together bust to bust; the men are in shirt-sleeves, the ladies in their ordinary frocks. The formal stuff is saved for the last night

The Shangri-Las are standing on stage in Pearly King and Queen outfits

Phil (*going to the microphone*) Ladies and gentlemen, take your partners please for the tango.

They switch on a tape recorder

Music—a tango

The tango begins and they start off leading the dance. They are excellent dancers and cover a great deal of the floor. Jimmy and Joan are also very good, as are Henry and Maureen. Pat is dancing with Jessie, Kathleen with "Evelyn". Everybody takes it all very seriously. Debbie and Clare and the Driver could perhaps dance with dolls in the shadows to give the impression of more people. The music stops and the couples freeze except for those actors talking

Pat I feel right stupid, you know.
Jessie What do you mean?
Pat Well, dancing bust to bust like this. I just feel daft.
Jessie Well it's better than sitting on your own.
Pat I suppose so.
Jessie Arthur were a lovely dancer weren't he? Oh, I'm sorry, Pat I've done it again.
Pat You're right love, don't worry, it's all right. Ay, he were a good dancer Arthur. He loved a good dance. This were one of his favourites.

Jessie The square tango.
Pat Ay, he loved it. We met at a dance.
Jessie Where?
Pat In Warrington. He was in the RAF and I was packing parachutes. It was nineteen forty-two, there was a dance on at the Baths. I was dancing with this big American sergeant, from Texas he was. He had proper cowboy boots on. He were massive, nearly seven foot.
Jessie Oooh I say!
Pat I couldn't understand a word he said, his mouth were full of chewing gum. Anyway the dance started up and Arthur came up and grabbed hold of me and that was that. He walked me home that night, all the way to my billet, he missed his bus, twelve miles he had to go back to his camp. They put him on a charge the next day but from then on we were hardly ever apart, four kids in six years, and we just got them off us hands and ... I don't know.
Jessie Never mind, love.

They dance on. The music stops and they sit down

Maureen You all right Pat?
Pat Yes thanks, I'm havin' a real time.
Jimmy Anybody ready for another drink?
Maureen Lager and lime please.
Jessie Snowball please, Jim.
Kathleen I'm all right, thank you.
Henry (*to anybody*) All spring maple this floor. The planks come from American Air Force Officers' Mess at Kidleford. In nineteen fifty-three it were knocked down.
Maureen Jim said what are you havin', Henry—a lager?

Henry nods

Joan Snowball please, Jim.
Jimmy Alice, Ede—a drink?
Pat I'll have a large brandy.
Kathleen Well I'm glad I'm not putting her to bed.
Pat You never know, a couple more brandies and I won't give a monkey's who puts me to bed. (*Winking*) Eh Jim?
Jimmy (*laughing and going off for the drinks; singing*) "There were three in the bed and the little one said roll over".
Phil Right lads and lasses. On the floor for one of your all-time favourites. The Slush.

Music—"The Slush"

The dancers get up to do "The Slush" and "The Dicky-bird" "Knock 3 Times"). As the evening progresses, the characters of the two entertainers emerge. Phil and Edna take off the pearly jackets to reveal Hawaiian shirts and garlands. They put on some romantic songs with Hawaiian guitars. While smiling at everybody they talk out of the corners of their mouths

   We vary the mood as the sun sinks slowly into the west and the dredger sinks slowly in the bay.

Music—"Hawaiian"

Act I, Scene 7   13

Edna I hate this music. You know I do.
Phil There's nowt wrong with it. It's a good music to dance to.
Edna It gets right on my nerves.
Phil Well I can't help your nerves. Anyway, the punters love it.
Edna That just goes to show how thick they are. (*She smiles at the dancers*)
Phil So just because they're enjoying themselves they're thick are they? You want a bit more bloody charity you do. Are we going to dance with them or not?
Edna I suppose we'll 'ave to.
Phil Ay and just remember—it's being so cheerful pays the bloody wages. Come on—buck up for God's sake!

They get off the stage. Edna goes over to Henry and gets him up to dance. Phil goes to Pat

(*To Pat*) Ey up love you've got a face like dip. Has someone died or summat?
Kathleen Yes, her husband.
Phil (*taken back by what he realizes was a stupid mistake, answering in all seriousness*) Eh, I'm sorry, love. It was only meant as a joke.
Pat No, you're right, love, you weren't to know and I was bloody miles away, stood by a piece of bloody Co-op marble in Barnsley cemetery, I was, and it won't bloody do. So come on, I'll have a dance with you.

They dance a slow waltz to the obvious displeasure of Kathleen and Maureen although Jessie, simple soul that she is, smiles happily as they pass and waves. Again, the music stops to allow the dialogue to come across

Phil I'm sorry about that love, how long ago was it?
Pat Nearly nine months now, but I'm getting over it bit by bit, you do, don't you?

They dance off and the music stops again. Cut to Kathleen

Kathleen (*spitefully*) She shouldn't have come, not with Arthur only dead just over the eight months.
Maureen Or at least she shouldn't be dancing the way she is.
Jessie What do you mean?
Kathleen Act your age.

Maureen and Kathleen just give each other knowing looks. Phil and Pat dance back on

Phil Were you happy together?
Pat Oh ay, he were a good man, a right good laugh he were. He always came on these dos.
Phil It's the first time we've worked Whitby. We used to work Scarborough and Brid a lot but we've never worked Whitby before.
Pat I thought we hadn't seen you before.
Phil What did he do, your husband?
Pat Arthur? He were a collier after he came out of the RAF, he was down the pit from nineteen forty-seven till three years last Christmas. He got miner's lung.

Phil That's bad that.
Pat It developed into cancer in the end. He took three years to die. It were obscene that. To see a fit man like that shrivel up and rot before your eyes. A dog shouldn't have to die like that.
Phil There's not much I can say, is there?
Pat No love, but you're listening and that helps. In fact, you're a very good listener.

Pat laughs and the waltz ends at that spot with the two of them standing under the mirror ball. The action freezes for a moment and as they look into each other's eyes there is a moment of understanding. The light passes across Kathleen's frozen face, Maureen's cold stare, Jessie's good-natured smile, Jim's quizzical look and the hard stare of Edna about to change the tape. A hard fade to black

SCENE 8

The beach

Seagulls calling and waves on the beach. A grey light slowly washes the stage. Back projection of a sea horizon

Pat is walking along the beach. As she walks we hear the sound of a hammer and see a man's figure. She is about to walk on, but something in the man's manner stops her. She moves closer and we see it is Phil

Pat Now then! So this is where you come to mend your boots is it?
Phil Oh, hallo love! Nay I'm not cobbling me shoes, I'm looking for ammonites.
Pat And what's one of them when it's at home? It sounds like an American religion. "Brethren, the Ammonite Church of California welcomes you today. One hundred dollars buys you a place in heaven. Send your money now and guarantee yourself a place in the Ammonite Tabernacle Choir."
Phil (*laughing, showing her a split pebble*) That's one, and that's one cut in half.
Pat What are they?
Phil They were creatures swimming in the seas millions of years ago. Then they died and got trapped in the mud and over millions of years they turned into this. A fossil.
Pat (*seriously*) So it's been locked in there all these millions of years.
Phil Ay, but I've let it out now.
Pat That's like us.
Phil What?
Pat We're like bloody fossils aren't we, living bloody fossils going through the motions never changing.
Phil (*laughing*) Ay, I suppose we are.
Pat (*breaking out of the mood*) Is it your hobby?
Phil Collecting fossils? No, not really. I'm interested in all sorts of things. I've got what I suppose you'd call a butterfly mind. I read about these in a book so I went and bought a rock hammer. I give 'em to the kids.

Act I, Scene 8

Pat Your grandchildren?
Phil No, any kids I meet. We haven't got any grandchildren. We only had one son and he were killed.
Pat What happened?
Phil Motor-bike crash. We called him Tom, my lad, after me brother. He got killed at Tobruk, our Tom. Broke me mother's heart. He were a grand lad, our son. He grew up tall, fit, good-looking, a good sportsman, passed for grammar school, got his O levels and A levels and went to university.
Pat He did well then?
Phil Ay, he got to Oxford. English he were studying. He loved reading, he were never without a book in his hand. His mother wanted him to be an engineer. "What's the use of English?" she said. "Get a degree in science or something." Anyway he took English and passed with a first-class degree. (*He pauses, he is obviously pained by the recollection*)

They stop walking

I were that proud of him! I thought—he's done it! He's done what I should have done. So I knew he were mad on motor bikes and I bought him one. She didn't want him to have it, but I did. Three weeks later he were hit by a car head-on. It was the driver's fault, but that doesn't bring him back. It took him three days to die.

They carry on walking

All those years of looking after them, bringing them up, making sure they don't fall over, stopping them falling in the fire. It seems such a waste. (*There are tears in his eyes*) Anyway, that were the end of it for both of us, she clammed up and went rock solid.
Pat But how have you managed to carry on working together?
Phil Force of habit, like you said, we're like fossils. The Shangri-Las, preserved for eternity. (*He laughs*) Aren't we bloody morbid?

They both laugh and walk on

How many kids have you got, Pat?
Pat Four, two boys and two girls. The eldest lad's an engineer in Australia. The two girls were in the middle, one's married and living in Aberdeen. Her husband works on the oil rigs. The other's nursing in Manchester and the youngest boy's a doctor in London. He's married. I've got five grandchildren altogether. We get together at Christmas and have a reight good do. But apart from that I hardly see them, they have their own lives to lead.
Phil Ay, it's funny really. You look after them all that time—then as soon as they're ready they fly the nest.
Pat Where do you live?
Phil Alfreton, near Derby.

They both start to walk

Pat Oh, it's not too far is it?
Phil No, not really.
Pat So you have a lot of hobbies, then?

Phil Well I do really, you see in this job you have to have something to fill your days in or you'd go potty staring at the bloody hotel walls.
Pat What does your wife do?
Phil (*a touch of acid in his voice*) Stares at the bloody hotel walls.

They turn and look at each other, then dropping their coats to reveal their costumes beneath, they come together and dance off

Scene 9

The ballroom. Night

The ballroom is full of dancers

Phil and Pat dance in. Phil, dressed as a cowboy, picks up his hat en passant

Edna is dressed as a cowgirl. The dancers are doing a barn dance. Pat and Phil split up and Pat dances with Jessie. Each time Pat and Jessie pass the stage Phil smiles at her and she smiles back. The dance finishes

Phil (*on the microphone*) Well folks, that's the end of the Gay Gordons—now it's Latin American time once more. Will you take your partners please for the square tango.

Music—"It's Now or Never"

Phil and Edna, as per usual, go to members of the opposite sex and take them on to the floor. Phil makes straight for Pat, an obvious move that no-one misses. Again, the music stops and starts to allow the dancers to deliver their lines

Phil I want to see you afterwards.

They dance

Pat (*as though she'd been expecting it*) Where?
Phil By the roundabout on the front at half-past twelve.
Pat What for?
Phil I want to talk to you.
Pat (*looking him straight in the eyes*) All right, I'll be there.

They dance on

Kathleen (*dancing with Maureen*) Well, he's making it very obvious what he's after.
Maureen That Edna must be able to see what's going on.

They look to where Edna is dancing with "Sid"

Kathleen She must be mad encouraging him like that. Everybody can see what's going on.

They dance on

Jimmy (*dancing with Joan*) You know, I think Phil's clicked with Pat.

Act I, Scene 9

Joan I hope she knows what she's doing. His wife's watching him like a hawk.
Jimmy Come on love, it's only a bit of fun.
Joan I'm not so sure.

They dance

Pat Are you serious?
Phil It's about the most serious thing I've ever said to anyone.
Pat Well, I don't know, it all seems so sudden in a way.
Phil (*as the dance ends*) Anyway we'll talk about it later. Half-twelve, on the pier.
Edna (*staring hard at them both*) Now ladies and gentlemen, it's time for the spot dance. Some lovely prizes, the giant Dumbo's still to go and there's a bottle of spirits and two bottles of wine for second and third.

Music—"Waltz in My Heart"

SCENE 10

The pier

As the dancers move upstage dancing, part of the forestage becomes the pier suggested by lighting, the shadow of ironwork and a back projection of the moon on the sea. The young couple we saw before at the Abbey are leaning on the railing looking out to sea and cuddling

Phil and Pat enter separately

Phil I didn't think you'd come.
Pat Why not?
Phil I don't know, I just didn't think you'd come.
Pat I think we both knew I would. There are some things that are so simple they don't need many words, Phil, and what's happening with us isn't something that needs a lot of talk.
Phil No, you're right. It was that first night when we were dancing. It was the way we looked at each other. You know the song, "Be sure it's true when you say I love you, it's a sin to tell a lie"? Well, I felt there was so much I wanted to say to you and yet at the same time I felt I didn't need to say it, almost as though you knew.
Pat I know, I felt that way too.
Phil I could feel it like—like electricity. Do you know what I felt more than anything else? Do you know what went through me that first night, like an electric shock?
Pat What?
Phil Joy, sheer bloody joy. Like every cell in my body were shouting halle-bloody-lujah. That's what I felt, I felt alive for the first time in years. I felt like—me again.

They look at the moon on the water

Pat So what are we going to do about it?
Phil I don't know. All my life it's been me and Edna, "The Shangri-Las". Edna, for twenty-five years she's been like a bloody hump on my back, and now you've come along. And I just don't know what to do.
Pat There's not a lot left for us is there? Not a lot of happiness, I mean. We can stay as fossils stuck in the stone forever if we want to, or maybe we can break out.
Phil It's not that easy is it. I suppose we're gettin' a bit old for this sort of carry on. Look at them. (*Nodding towards the young couple*) They're just starting off in life, two kids on the edge of the pool, waiting to dive in, we've got it all behind us.
Pat I saw them at the Abbey, they must be on honeymoon.
Phil It must be wonderful to be young like that.
Pat Rubbish!
Phil What?
Pat What's the difference? We might not be twenty-one in our bodies but in our souls we're no different, not inside we aren't, we're twenty-one, we're seventeen, we're whatever we want to be, Phil.
Phil (*looking at her with a deeper understanding*) Ay, you're right. You're so bloody right.

They move closer together and very tenderly and very lovingly they kiss and hold each other tight

What are we going to do?
Pat What do you want to do?
Phil I want you, Pat. I may have only known you for a few days but I know for certain I want you. Whatever's left of my life, I want to spend it with you. But how the hell can we?
Pat What's to stop us? You're a good man, Phil, I can tell. We can be happy together. We've just got to make the break. Like the fossils. We've got to crack the stone. I'm free, I've got nobody to hurt. I've got nobody, but what about Edna?
Phil She wouldn't miss me. Not really. We don't even enjoy working together any more. (*Pause*) Pat, let's go away together.
Pat Where to?
Phil Have you got your own place?
Pat Yes, I've got my own house. It's only small, there's not much to it, but we can't go there, not at the moment, not for a bit at least. I've still got Arthur's mother living with us. It wouldn't be right to go there. Not straight away it wouldn't. I've got a sister in Sunderland. We could perhaps go there for a bit, while we sorted ourselves out.
Phil Would she have us?
Pat Ay, probably. She's a bit of a mad bugger like me. We could go to our Kitty's. What about Edna?
Phil She'll be mad—I know she will. But it won't be love or jealousy, it'll be because she's losing something, a possession, something she sees as hers. I've not been a person to her for years. (*Pause*) Pat, I do love you. And I want you so much.

Act I, Scene 10   19

Pat I love you too, Phil. You know Phil, whatever happens I'll always remember this night. I think we've got a chance of happiness. It's up to us to go for it. But it won't half cause some bother you know.

Music—"Falling in Love Again"

Then, very tenderly, they kiss in the moonlight

CURTAIN

ACT II

Scene 1

The ballroom

Music—a tango

The "stage" area contains a number of small prizes. Jessie, Kathleen and Maureen are sitting, the rest are backstage getting ready

Phil (*on the microphone as Jimmy Savile*) Well guys and gals, it's talent night at the *Royal Hotel* and our prizes, courtesy of the management, are a meal for two at the Blue Lagoon, oh, I don't fancy that, a bottle of sherry and a sand picture of the Queen. The corner's been knocked off and one of her eyes' slipped but it's nothing that a bit of Araldite can't mend. So guys and gals, as it 'appens—I'll pass you over to Edna who'll announce the contestants.
Kathleen Who is it he is supposed to be taking off?
Maureen It's Tarzan.
Kathleen Oh you mean that 'Eseltine.
Edna And our first contestants on tonight's "Search for a Star" are Jimmy, Joan and Pat as "Sons of the Desert".

She turns to Phil, who is struggling with the tape deck

Phil The tape's jammed.
Edna (*nastily*) Well, get a bloody move on.

Music—Wilson, Kepple and Betty

The music jerks into life and Jimmy, Joan and Pat come on from L. *They do a full version of the sand dance, then exit to applause*

The music finishes

During the next, Pat, Joan and Jimmy come on and sit down

Phil That was the "Sons of the Desert" there, ladies and gentlemen, although unless my eyes have totally gone two of them were appearing under false pretences. Now, ladies and gentlemen, an act of special value, two for the price of one. You don't often get that these days. Put your hands together for the two tapping twins from Twinderon, Alice and Edie.

Music as Alice and Edie perform their dance, then exit to applause

Now, the moment you've all been waiting for. At great expense, he's just

Act II, Scene 1

returned from a summer season at Kensington Working Men's Club, a retired tripe dresser from Cleckheaton to give you a burst of percussive paradiddles on the cow's shin-bones, Henry McCalman.

Henry comes on stage in kilt and sporran. He cranks up an old wind-up gramophone circa 1930 and plays the bones in time to the "William Tell Overture" or the "Radetsky March". The gramophone keeps winding down and Henry has to keep running back from the microphone to wind it up. This is all part of the act. He does it with a totally straight face. It should go on as long as the audience will stand it. Finally the spring breaks on the gramophone and it goes faster and faster until Henry's fingers are a blur and the bones fly off in different directions. He finishes to applause

Phil Wonderful, wonderful. If only that cow knew it was going to end up in show business. Give him a big hand, guys and gals. Right, now Jessie is going to give us a song—with me doing a turn on the organ, can't be bad, can it.

Cheers and claps follow, some of them ribald

Jessie (*getting up to sing*) What did he say about doing a turn?
Kathleen Something filthy.
Jessie I missed it.
Kathleen Good job.
Phil Ladies and gentlemen, let's have a really big Whitby welcome for Jessie.

Jessie has a sweet soprano voice. She sings "When You Were Sweet Sixteen" beautifully, and Phil accompanies her on the organ

Music—"When You Were Sweet Sixteen"

We are aware that the girls from the dining-room have crept in and are leaning on the door jamb (or on a pillar) listening. By the end of the song they are both wiping tears from their eyes. They exit shortly

Pat, too, sits staring into space. Applause and Jessie sits down smiling happily

Pat That was beautiful, Jessie.
Kathleen Very nice. Sit down.
Joan (*to Pat*) You all right love?
Pat (*smiling*) Ay. (*Pause*) That were Arthur's favourite. He would have liked it tonight.
Jimmy You were nearly as good as him tonight, weren't she Joan?
Joan Proper star she was.
Pat Only me legs aren't as hairy as his were. Arthur would have laughed. He always said I had nice legs.
Jimmy You're not getting upset, are you?
Pat No, I'm over it now. I knew in the middle of this week I'd laid him to rest. He's at peace now. Something happened, I just felt him here with us, laughing at something and felt release sort of. I suppose it's silly really. But I felt him wanting me to have a good time, I felt him behind me saying, "Go on enjoy yourself". Sounds daft, doesn't it.

Joan No, it's not silly.
Pat What would he have said, Jimmy?
Jimmy Nay, gi'o'er you're a long time dead, get supped up, give us a smile and gerrum in.

They laugh

Beams of light spin from the mirror ball. Kathleen's face is as miserable as before, Maureen coldly blank and Jessie warm and open as ever

Edna Ladies and gentlemen, would you take your partners please for the St Bernard's Waltz.

Music — St Bernard's Waltz

Henry Come on, Mo. Off we go.
Maureen Not me. I'm sitting this one out. Go and dance with Edna.
Henry (*to Edna*) May I have this dance?
Jessie Are we getting up?
Kathleen I'm not. I think I've got a bunion coming up. I don't know what I pay that chiropodist for.
Jessie I didn't know your feet were private.
Kathleen I didn't mind going on the National Health for my (*she points down at her stomach and drops her voice a tone, almost matching the word*) hysterectomy, but your feet are different. There's some bits you can lose and not miss much but your feet are with you for ever. You don't need a (*she drops a tone on the word*) womb — well, not to go shopping.
Jessie (*in all innocence*) Or ride a bike.

Kathleen gives her a look

Come on, Maureen.
Maureen (*to Kathleen*) Shall I?
Kathleen You can if you want.
Maureen I don't know.
Jessie Come on.
Kathleen Oh go on, she'll mither you to death.
Maureen Oh all right.

They get up. The dance commences and as before the other dancers freeze as the main action comes downstage and the actors deliver their lines

Henry Do you know, nineteen forty-four when Jerry bombed Hull, one of their bombers going home dropped a bomb on Whitby.
Edna (*truly bored*) That's interesting.
Henry Landed right on the pickle works. Petulengro's Gypsy Orchestra were at the Spa that night. It blew all the windows in and although the drummer were temporarily blinded by a flying gherkin, he never lost a beat.
Edna (*sarcastically*) Do you know, Henry, you should write a book?
Henry I have done.

They dance off and Pat and Phil dance forward

Act II, Scene 1   23

Phil Did you manage to phone your sister?
Pat Yes. She said we can go and stay with her till we get ourselves sorted out. She thought it were right funny. (*Pause*) I'm scared, Phil—it won't be easy.
Phil Nothing worth having ever is. (*He kisses Pat on the neck*)

They exit

Edna (*switching off the tape*) Thank you, ladies and gentlemen. That concludes another fun-filled evening with "The Shangri-Las". I hope we shall have the pleasure of your company tomorrow night. Thank you and good-night.
Kathleen We haven't even had the Last Waltz.
Edna I'm sorry. Good-night.
Kathleen But you can't finish without the Last Waltz.
Edna Well you can have two tomorrow night.

She exits

Henry I think it's because I stepped on her foot.
Maureen I am not having this, we've paid our money.
Jimmy Come on, Joan, let's have another go at sixty-nine.
Jessie Oh, have you had another French letter?

They exit

Maureen Aren't you coming, Henry?
Henry I'll just finish me fag.

Maureen exits after the others

Debbie enters to wipe down the table with a cloth

Debbie Sorry, but I've been told to clear up in here.
Henry That's all right, luv. Weren't you here last year?
Debbie Yes, and the rate I'm going I'll be here next bloody year.
Henry You should get a job at the *Royal* in Scarborough. That's a wonderful hotel. Have you ever been there?
Debbie Can't say I have. I tend more towards Henry Africa's on my nights off.
Henry (*ignoring her*) When I were stationed at Catterick I used to come over every leave on me motor-bike to the *Royal*. I'd stop at a little guest house near the Happy Valley, leave me dancing things there, the old lady who ran it used to look after them for me—lovely kippers she did, proper Craster Kippers they were—I never had heartburn at all in them days. I could drink Guinness and eat kippers till they were comin' out of me ears—not now though, one smell of a kipper and I'm doubled up like a clothes peg and burpin' like a five hundred cc Norton—Troy and his Manoliers were on for three weeks in nineteen thirty-nine—lovely band they were. I met a Land Army girl there one night. She was lovely with masses of red hair all the way down to her bum. We courted steady for nearly six months. I would have married her only she ran off with a pig man from Bridlington—reserved occupation you see—pig farmers.

Debbie (*genuinely saddened*) Aw, that's really sad.
Henry (*without realizing the* double entendre) Ay, he could slip her the pork you see.

Gino enters in full chef's uniform, wiping his hands on a towel hanging from his waist

Debbie (*loudly and clearly*) Gino, there's a parcel for you at Reception. It's been there since yesterday. Mandy forgot to give it to you last night. Gino, that recipe you gave me mum for spaghetti à la vongole was really good. She was dead pleased with it. (*Louder*) Dead pleased.
Henry (*sensing an opportunity*) Eh! Buena note Gino. Com estas. Me parliamo poco Italiano. In guera secondo mondiale este in Monte Casino. Multo soldatas Deutch. Multo amigos mortas. Multo senoritas in trattoria, multo vino, multo cantos. Amore, amore. Multo bambinos.
Gino (*to Debbie*) What the bleedin' hell is he on about?
Henry I thought you were Italian.
Gino (*shouting*) Me mam and dad are. I were born in Bradford.

He exits

Debbie He's not Italian—he's deaf.

Henry exits

Clare enters

Clare Oh. That's not your new boyfriend is it? Hey, there's a right row going on upstairs.
Debbie Why, what's happened?
Clare That Edna's tearing round the corridor looking for Phil. There's smoke coming out of her ears. And that Kathleen, you know, the big one with the face like a box of frogs, she's sulking because she hasn't had a Last Waltz.
Debbie Well you always have to have the Last Waltz. Come on, we've got the place to ourselves. (*On mike*) Ladies and gentlemen, take your partners please for the Geriatric Gavotte.

Music—waltz

Come on, Phil and Edna, eat your hearts out.

They waltz off

The Lights crossfade to the beach

SCENE 2

The beach

Pat Hallo love.
Phil Hallo smiler.

Act II, Scene 2

They kiss

Are you all right?
Pat (*smiling*) Ay, I was just going for a walk.
Phil I saw you go out. Where are the rest of them?
Pat I couldn't stand the looks.
Phil What looks?
Pat From Kathleen mainly. She doesn't think I should be dancing.
Phil With me?
Pat With anybody really. She pulls faces and talks about me behind me back, I know. Mind you, that Kathleen will never be happy as long as her arse looks at the ground. She knows something's going on, I can tell.
Phil Do you think what she thinks important?
Pat Well, you can't help but let it upset you when they're talking behind your back about you but in the end I just think, bugger them, I'll do what I think's right.
Phil Well do it. Whatever you think's right. You're a long time dead you know. This is not a rehearsal.
Pat Funny, Arthur used to say that.
Phil You miss him a lot, don't you?
Pat Of course I do, he was more than just a husband, he was a friend. But I'm learning the difference between missing someone and being sick with grief. Grief's good and it does you good to grieve but too much and it can be like jealousy or hate—it can eat you away like acid.
Phil You must have loved him very much.
Pat Ay, we both loved each other. We had our ups and downs, who doesn't, but he never betrayed me. There was never a time when he wasn't my friend and the same went for me. (*Pause*) Were you ever happy, Phil?
Phil Yes, we were at first. We got on well, she was a good mother. The house was spotless, there was always a meal on the table and all that, but we haven't really spoken to each other for ten years and we haven't lived together as man and wife for fifteen.
Pat What went wrong, was it the lad dying?
Phil I think we were already drifting apart. I suppose we married too young or something. But the lad dying killed it all for us. She blamed me, said it was my fault. He was the only one, see. She had a hard time having him so she wouldn't have any more. I wanted a big family but that's the way it is. You have to cut your coat according to your cloth.

They come across a dead seagull by a pool. Phil kneels down to it

Pat What is it?
Phil A dead seagull.
Pat Poor little thing.
Phil There was a man called Icarus once, did you ever read about him?

Pat shakes her head

In Greek mythology it was. He tried to fly.
Pat What?

Phil He made wings out of wax and feathers and he flew.
Pat What happened?
Phil He flew towards the sun. He got too near and his wings melted. The wax softened, the feathers came apart and he fell back down to earth.
Pat Some of us are like that too.
Phil Try to fly too high?
Pat No. Some of us are just trying to fly. Still I'd rather go like that than stay a fossil all my life.

Music—"When I Grow Too Old to Dream"

A gull calls and they come together and waltz slowly off into the sea-wrack, disappearing from view as . . .

The other dancers waltz on into . . .

Scene 3

The ballroom again. Night

It's fancy dress night. Maureen is dressed as a harem girl, Kathleen as Britannia and Jessie is dressed up as a rag doll. Jimmy and Joan are dressed as Laurel and Hardy. There are various King Kongs, Arab sheikhs, belly dancers, Kojaks (women with bald masks on), etc. They dance around long enough for Pat and Phil to change their costumes

Phil enters, dressed as a clown, and goes to the microphone

Phil Right, ladies and gentlemen. Time for the fancy dress parade. Line up over by the far column and we'll parade round to the *March of the Mods*.

There is a noise from the back of the ballroom, Phil looks over. We follow his point of vision and realize why people are laughing

Pat enters, dressed as Mae West, with an enormous pair of false breasts

Pat Come up and see me sometime.

Music—"March of the Mods"

Pat joins the procession and when they get in front of the stage, they line up. We see, but nobody else does, Pat drop a plastic turd in the middle of the dance floor and as the fancy dress contestants line up in front of the stage they see it. The reaction is varied. Most of the women laugh uproariously, as do the men. Kathleen, however, glares at it blackly, Maureen thinks it is real and Jessie looks at it open-mouthed

Maureen Eugh!! It's dog dirt!
Jessie (*seriously, looking at a man who's come dressed as a dog*) He didn't do it, did he?
Kathleen If this is someone's idea of a joke I don't think it's funny.
Edna (*coming down from the stage and walking over to it*) Some people who think they have a sense of humour really only have a filthy mind.

Act II, Scene 3

Laughing, Phil jumps from the stage and picks it up. He walks over to Pat and gives it to her

Phil I've a good mind to rub your nose in it.

Pat laughs and puts it back in her handbag

Jimmy (*laughing*) Get down Shep.
Henry That's a fair pair of buzzies you've got there.
Pat They're real, you know. (*Peeling down the front of her dress to reveal the enormous plastic breasts*) How about that, Henry? I bet you wouldn't like one of those on your nose for a wart.

There is raucous laughter. Phil and Edna go back on to the stage. They are about to announce the winners of the fancy dress competition. Edna is looking down her nose at Pat

Phil (*on the microphone*) Right ladies and gentlemen, the results of the fancy dress are as follows. Third prize goes to Mae West——

There are cheers, etc.

—second prize goes to the dog——

More cheers

—and the first prize goes to Laurel and Hardy.

Cheers, etc., prizes are given out very quickly and congratulations given

Now take your partners for the foxtrot, "Love Locked Out".

Edna goes to the tape machine and switches it on

Music—"Love Locked Out"

Jessie We are all on the game, Mo.
Edna (*nodding towards Pat*) She's a coarse cow.
Phil You'd know, would you?
Edna She's common as muck.
Phil She was just having a laugh, that's all, it was only a bit of fun.
Edna You're not fooling anyone, you know. (*She smiles at someone dancing past as she says this and waves, talking out of the corner of her mouth*)
Phil What do you mean? (*He smiles and waves at someone else passing*)

The dancers gradually leave the stage during the remainder of this scene

Edna There's something going on between you and her. I can tell, I haven't been married to you for this long without being able to read you like a book. It's just like that red-head in Llandudno. Well, I'll tell you what (*waving at someone and smiling*) you can have her and good riddance to you.
Phil I might just do that. (*He smiles and waves*)
Edna Well, don't think I'd miss you, 'cos I wouldn't. I wouldn't even know you'd be gone. (*She waves at somebody going past*)

Phil You don't have to tell me. It's been like living with a waxwork for twenty-five years.
Edna Well, you know what you can do then, don't you! And the sooner the better.
Phil Ay, I just bloody well might do that too.

They come together and dance off

Jimmy There's something going on I can tell. There's an atmosphere. There's going to be trouble.
Joan Well, there's nothing we can do about it. She's a big girl now. The best thing we can do is just stick around.
Jimmy And pick up the pieces.
Joan That's what friends are for.

They dance off

Maureen You don't know how lucky you are, Jessie, never having married.
Jessie Oh Maureen, Henry's nice.
Maureen It's not 'im so much. It's the way he carries on. You'd think sex'd stop at fifty-odd but not him—he still thinks he's twenty-one.
Jessie Ooh Maureen. You shouldn't be telling me.
Maureen It's all right. It doesn't get him anywhere. I told him ten years ago. I've done my share. When you feel like that you can go and dig your allotment.

Pause

Jessie You did have some lovely shallots last year.

They dance off

Scene 4

The tearoom. The afternoon of the next day

The two tea girls dance on pushing the counter and tea urn

Pat dances in on her own

Kathleen, Maureen and Jessie dance in a little after

Kathleen Here she is, hiding away on her own.
Jessie Are you all right, Pat?
Pat Ay, I just wanted a bit of a think, that's all.

They all sit down and order tea. There is a strained silence

Kathleen Jessie, sit down and shut up. Can we have some service here please. I didn't think what you did last night was funny.
Pat Didn't you, Kathleen? Well, I didn't think you would. I only did it for a joke you know. It was a bit of fun, do you remember, fun, or is it too long ago that you had any?

Act II, Scene 4

Kathleen Well, I didn't think it was funny. It was coarse and vulgar.
Pat (*getting angry but staying calm*) No, well we'll just have to differ on that point then, won't we. I am coarse and vulgar and it's too late to change it now.
Kathleen And another thing.
Pat Oh, there's another thing is there?
Kathleen Yes there is. (Can we have some service please). We don't like the way you're carrying on with that Phil.
Pat Who doesn't?
Kathleen We don't.
Pat And what do you mean by carryin' on, anyway?
Kathleen You know quite well what I mean.
Pat No, I don't know what you mean. Dancing with him? Do you mean that? Because if you do mean that there's been a lot of carrying on going on. I danced with Jessie once or twice. I'm not having an affair with her you know.
Jessie No, she certainly is not!
Kathleen You know what I mean full well. You've been carrying on with him. You were seen out with him on the pier.
Pat Who by?
Jessie It was me. I had one of me heads and I was walking near there when I saw you.

The waitress enters

I didn't mean to cause a row, Pat, honest.
Kathleen Just hold your horses, you.
Pat Well listen, all three of you. Not that it's any of your business, which it isn't, but Phil and me are in love.

Kathleen shrieks scornfully so that the waitresses look round from behind the tea urns

Kathleen In love! In love!
Pat Ay, do you remember the feeling, Kathleen?
Maureen But you've only known him a week!
Pat How long does it take to know that you're in love with somebody? A year? Two years? A lifetime? Two minutes? A split second? You were married thirty-seven years, Kathleen, were you in love? You hardly spoke to him for the last ten years.
Jessie Ten years.
Kathleen That's got nothing to do with it. You're mad you are, carrying on like a big soft kid and (*taking her hankie out and wiping her eyes*) Arthur hardly in his grave. How could you do it? How could you?
Pat Arthur's been dead nine bloody months. The dead are dead and gone and, as far as I know, don't give a toss about the living, and you can stop your bloody craw thumping and sniffling for Arthur, Kathleen, because Arthur couldn't bloody stand you. Do you know what he used to call you? The Bible Basher. And do you know what he would say if he were alive? "Get on with it, enjoy your bloody self", that's what he would say.

There is a silence. The tea girls are hanging on every word

Jessie What are you going to do, Pat?

Pat We're going to live together.

Maureen ⎱ *(together)* Live together.
Kathleen ⎰

Jessie Where?

Pat My sister's in Sunderland for a while.

Maureen Bloody hellfire!

Kathleen Oh my God!! She's gone mad.

Pat I haven't, I've done just the opposite, Kathleen. I've gone sane. I've woken up that's what I've done. I don't give a toss what anyone thinks or says. I'm going to enjoy the last years of me bloody life and so is Phil.

Kathleen You'll regret it.

Pat So what if I do? At least I'll have tried. I'll at least have done something instead of spending the rest of me life sitting talking about the price of bloody tins of corned beef in the Co-op. At least I won't end up a bleeding ammonite like you lot.

She storms out leaving the others in shocked amazement

The tea girl, nearly sniggering, comes to the table

Tea Girl Yes, ladies? Can I help you?

Jessie Yes, would you tell me what's a namonite?

The other two stare into the distance too numb to speak. Eventually they rise. Kathleen throws some money on the table

Kathleen Come on. I've got a phone call to make. I'm going to put a stop to this. She's not well. She needs help. She's only us as friends. We've got to do something! Jessie, come on.

Music—"Boy Next Door"

   They exit

Scene 5

A simple shelter on the prom

Gulls and waves. The light is mellowing as the sun sinks towards the west

Pat is sitting alone, a hankie in her hand, staring towards the sea

The young couple who were kissing on the pier walk past, arms wrapped around each other, kissing and whispering

Pat's eyes follow them

Jessie walks into the light. She is obviously looking for Pat

Jessie Oh Pat, I am glad I found you.

Pat It's OK, come and sit down.

Act II, Scene 5

Jessie (*sitting beside her*) I'm sorry, Pat love, I didn't mean to cause any mischief. I only told her I'd seen you on the pier 'cause I was a bit worried about you.
Pat (*sympathetically*) You needn't have worried, Jessie love. I'm a big girl now.
Jessie I'm sorry about Kathleen. I didn't want you to fall out.
Pat She's always been the same. Ever since we were little. You haven't known her as long as I have. It's not her fault she's the way that she is. Her mother was a nagger too. She couldn't play out with the rest of us when she were a kid. We were all too rough for her. They had her walkin' round town bangin' the bloody Temperance drum when she were twelve years old and givin' out leaflets outside the pub on a Saturday night. It's enough to twist anybody is that. Then when she got married it wasn't any better, a Methodist lay preacher and corner-shop grocer. You could have drowned his brains in a thimble. I don't think they were ever happy together. They just drifted along together like two sticks going down a river and out to the tide. There was no real love there. Just two people used to each other and too frightened of loneliness to break it all off. But loneliness isn't being alone. Loneliness is being married to someone you don't love. That's the worst sort of loneliness there is. Because you don't share things, you don't talk things out. You're just two empty shells rattlin' against each other. That was one of the good things about Arthur. He'd never let me mope. "Come on me duck," he'd say. "You've got a face like dip. Let's get the kettle on and have a cup of tea and talk it out." He always said that holding things inside were like screwin' a lid down on a boiling kettle—somethin' had to burst sometime.
Jessie I can talk to Twink and Muffin. They know when I'm upset.
Pat I know you can, love.
Jessie They might be only animals but they know what I'm feeling. They know when I'm upset.
Pat It's the most important thing there is, is love, Jessie. If you've ever known what it's like then it's difficult to do without it. It's not sex. I'm not talkin' about that, though that's important. It's feelin' close to somebody, real close; feeling his arms round you, yours round him, cuddling up together in bed. Having a friend. A real friend, the closest friend you've got, someone who'll never let you down. It's all that and more is love, whether it's woman to man, man to man, woman to woman, it's all one you know.
Jessie What d'you mean, woman to woman? Are you talking about them, what d'you call them, lesbians? I think it's awful, all of that.
Pat It's not. It's only love, Jessie. If two people love each other and care for each other, really care for each other, does it matter what sex they are or what they do in bed? To love, to care for, to make each other happy—it's so important. We've such little time and happiness is like a little candle that lights us on our way through the dark. We've got to love, Jessie. We weren't meant to be alone, not really. It's the most wonderful thing there is to open your front door and shout "I'm home!" and know that there's somebody there waiting for you that loves you and is really happy to see

you. If you've had that once, just once, then by Christ the world's the worst desert there is without it.

Jessie I've got my Twink and Muffin, they're always glad to see me. Anyway, not all marriages work out.

Pat Don't I know it. You see 'em all the time, the Henrys and Maureens of this world. Invisible to each other, carrying on carrying on. You know, if you take a goldfish out of its bowl after it's been in it for years and let it loose in a big tank, it just keeps on swimming round and round, round and round as though they're still in the bloody bowl. And that's what life is unless we do something to change it. We just go round and round and round in circles. Work, home, tea, television, bed. Work, home, tea, television, bed.

Jessie What can we do about it?

Pat We can break the soddin' bowl before it's too late!

Kathleen and Maureen appear out of the shadows, looking for Jessie

Maureen There she is.

Kathleen Where've you been? We've been looking for you all over the shop! We saw you weren't at afternoon tea and you weren't in your room.

Jessie I were sat here with Pat. We were just talkin'.

Kathleen Well she'll have plenty of talking to do soon.

Pat What's that supposed to mean?

Kathleen I've been on the phone to your Sally in Manchester.

Pat You've been what? What the hell has any of this got to do with you— you interfering bitch!

Kathleen Well, somebody had to tell her. She had a right to know. You're making a fool of yourself in front of everybody. Anyroad, she's on her way over from Manchester with John.

Jessie Oh Kathleen!

Maureen She did right.

Pat You wicked old cow.

Music—Military Two-step

Kathleen and Maureen dance off L, *Pat and Jessie off* R

Scene 6

The foyer

Henry is leaning against the reception desk boring the receptionist (Debbie or Clare). There is nobody else about

Jimmy and Joan enter the lobby area arm in arm. They look serious and concerned

Phil crosses the stage as they reach C. *He is obviously in a hurry*

Phil Hallo there, been a lovely day, hasn't it? You've been lucky with the weather.

Act II, Scene 6   33

He goes to pass but Jimmy reaches out a hand and gently stops him
Jimmy Just a minute, Phil—we want a bit of a word with you.
Joan We've heard the news.
Phil From Pat?
Jimmy No, we haven't had a chance to speak to her yet. We were just on our way to her room.
Phil (*laughing drily*) Hotels are like ships at sea, rumours and stories spread faster than fire, you can't keep a secret, can you?
Joan You've hardly made it a secret, either of you. Anyway, that's neither here nor there. It was Kathleen who told us—though we already knew that something more than a bit of fun was going on, didn't we love?
Jimmy Ay, we've known Pat for too long not to know how she's feeling. Listen, Phil. We both think the world of Pat. Our kids grew up together. I was down t' pit with Arthur. We've watched her struggle and we've watched her grieve and (*pause*) we don't want her being made a fool of now—not after what she's gone through.
Joan She's solid gold is that lass—through and through. You'll not find a better and if I thought you were buggerin' her about—I'd break your bloody neck meself!
Phil I know you're both worried for her—but you needn't be. She'll tell you herself that my marriage has been a joke for the last ten years but I'll tell you something now. I have played around, I've not been an angel. I've had one or two flings—and near misses. But this one is different. I felt something the moment I saw her and it's got stronger ever since. I've never felt such an intense happiness and love for somebody else before, not like this, ever. I know that it's only words and words can be twisted and turned into lies. But they're all we've got to use with each other and I'll tell you now in all honesty, using the simplest words I know—I love Pat. I don't know where the road's going to lead or what is in store, but I won't leave her or mess her about. I love her, pure and simple—and that's it.
Joan (*putting her arms around him and giving him a big hug; tearfully*) Look after her, Phil—please look after her.
Phil (*patting her*) I will do love, don't worry, I will.

Jimmy is deeply moved and tries clumsily to stuff his pipe to hide his confusion, losing half his baccy as he tries to shake Phil's hand which is still round Joan's waist

Jimmy Ay—well—(*lost for words*)—all the best Phil. We'll be thinking of you both.
Phil I'm sorry if I've spoiled your last night.
Jimmy Nay, you haven't. Take more than this to stop us dancin'—wouldn't it, love.
Joan Coach doesn't come till tomorrer anyway and we aren't going to sit in us rooms. Are we, love?
Jimmy Bugger that for a game of soldiers. Anyway, come on love, we'd best go and see Pat.
Joan Ay, I bet she's in a hell of a state. See you, Phil—take care.

Phil (*moving away*) Ay. See you when I see you.
Jimmy Ay see you, Phil—and take care of that lass. She's not as hard as you think.
Phil I know that. (*Pause*) See you.

He waves and exits

Jimmy and Joan turn to go to the rooms

Jimmy What a bloody carry-on. We get worse the bloody older we get.
Joan I'm goin' to have to watch you with that Edna—now she's a free spirit.
Jimmy (*turning to face her*) You what? Edna!! She's as much chance of shovin' butter up a porcupine's arse wi' a warm knittin' needle. (*Beat as he changes mood*) Poor lass though—she must be goin' through hell.

They exit

Henry Well yes, she said "Could you give me a little bit of petrol, only I've got some grease spots on me coat and I want to clean them off."

Edna enters from L with Phil

Edna Yes. I've heard all that before. You've humiliated me for the last time. I've had enough.
Phil You won't even talk about it.
Edna I don't want to talk to you. I want to talk to her.

She exits followed by Phil

Phil (*as he goes*) Will you listen to me.
Henry ... so, he syphoned some petrol off and off we goes. A week later we were going back off us holidays and the old woman, she must have been waiting for our coach because she flagged us down.

Kathleen enters from L with Maureen. Jessie enters from R

Kathleen There you are, Jessie. We've been looking all over for you. Where's Pat?
Jessie I don't know.
Kathleen I told you to keep an eye on her. Don't you ever do what you're told? She's probably with that Phil again.
Jessie Well, it's none of our business.
Kathleen Of course it's our business. She wants protection from herself. She's no consideration for other people. I mean Jessie, she's even coming between us. What's going to happen to our friendship.
Jessie I'll tell you what's going to happen to our friendship Kathleen. You can stick it up your bum.

Kathleen, dumbfounded, walks to exit, turns to Jessie

I've been waiting to say that for twenty-five years.

Kathleen and Maureen exit

Jessie exits

Act II, Scene 6   35

Henry As I was saying, seems like she had an accident with the petrol. She put some in a saucer to dab on her coat and forgot it was there and put some milk in it for the cat.

Sally enters

Debbie Can I help you?
Sally For God's sake John, what are you doing? Come on. (*To Debbie*) Can I speak to Mrs Amos please.
Debbie (*on tannoy*) Would Mrs Amos please come to Reception. Mrs Amos to Reception.

Pause

Henry So next . . .

Sally looks at Henry

Debbie It had run out of petrol.

John and Pat enter

Sally Where have you been?
John I was parking the car.

Henry is staring into space, bemused. He walks quietly away trying not to look foolish

Sally is pacing up and down. John is examining the wallpaper. Both of them are very twitchy

Pat enters

Pat Hallo love, hallo John. Who's minding Kylie and Justin?
John They're at my mother's.
Sally Mother! (*Kissing her*) What's been going on?
John We've been worried sick about you.
Pat Nothing's "going on" as you put it. I've just decided to change my life that's all.
John Who is this bloke?
Pat Listen John, I don't want to fall out with you, but when you married our Sally you didn't marry me.
Sally Mother, how long has this thing been going on?
Pat About a week.
Sally A week! You can't go off and live with somebody you've only known a week!
John I know it's nothing to do with me but I think you're making a fool of yourself.
Pat I'm not greatly worried what you think, John; and as for making a fool of myself—that's my choice isn't it.
Sally Mother, you're acting like a teenager!
Pat I know, and it's bloody marvellous!
Sally I've spoken to our Susan and she thinks you've gone mad. I've not phoned Australia yet but our Dave is furious!
Pat Isn't it bloody marvellous!

Sally What?

Pat Your mother's turned into a geriatric delinquent! Sally, neither I nor your father ever said a word to you about any of the lads you brought home——

Sally begins to look a bit uncomfortable

—even though some of them were basically pure rubbish. We didn't even say anything when you told us you were stoppin' at Tracey's and we knew you were sleepin' at that hippies' place in Mexborough.

Reaction from Sally and John—he obviously has never heard of this

We just watched over you and supported you. And that's the least you could do for me.

Sally Well I don't know what to say. Are you sure you know what you're doing?

Pat How can any of us ever really be sure they know what they're doing. I know what I want and I'm going into it with both my eyes wide open. In fact both of us are.

Sally But he's married!

Pat He's not been married for twenty-five years. He's got a piece of paper that says he and Edna share the same second name and that's all they share.

Sally What would me dad say?

Pat He'd tell me to get on with it, you know he would. He told you all he didn't want any mourning and moaning.

Sally But nine months, Mum.

Pat Nine months, nine years, nine centuries. What's time got to do with it?

John Where is he? We ought to see him.

Pat I'll tell you what you ought to do, John. You ought to get back in your car and drive back to Manchester. Stop in York on your way back. Have a nice meal, stay the night even. Treat our Sally. Enjoy yourself, do what you like BUT STAY OUT OF MY BLOODY LIFE. No Sally, I don't think it's a good idea for you to see Phil yet. Things are too much of a turmoil at present.

Sally What are you going to do?

Pat We're going to stay with our Auntie Kitty for a few days while we just sort things out. Then we'll just take things day by day—see where we go from there I suppose.

Sally I don't know what to say!

Pat In that case, say nowt. Just wish me luck.

Sally (*breaking down into tears and putting her arms round her*) I do Mum—I do. It's just that . . .

Pat (*fighting back the tears*) Look Sally. I'll be all right. Honestly! Don't worry about me. You and John get back into your car and go back to Manchester and look after those grandchildren of mine.

Sally and Pat dance off, followed by John, who dances

Kathleen enters

Act II, Scene 6

Kathleen (*to Debbie*) Have you seen Mrs Amos?
Debbie She has just gone into the dining-room to have some tea.
Kathleen Did she have a young couple with her?
Debbie Yes, she did.

Kathleen exits

Clare enters

Clare What's going on?
Debbie Well, Phil and Edna have had a row, that Pat has gone off with one of "The Shangri-Las" and all the other wrinklies are running all over the place, all hell is let loose.
Clare Bloody hell! You'd think they'd be past arguing at their age, wouldn't you. What are they going to do about tonight?
Debbie Edna says she doesn't care, she's not going to cancel it, she's going to do it on her own. She says she's glad to be rid of him.
Clare It seems a bit disgusting to me. You know, they're too old for that sort of thing really.
Debbie I think it's dead funny.

Mrs Mingham enters (or vox off)

Mrs Mingham Deborah! Clare!
Debbie We were just talking, Mrs Mingham.
Mrs Mingham Well, talk your way through those breakfast settings and be quick about it.
Debbie ⎫
Clare ⎭ (*together*) Yes, Mrs Mingham.

They exit

Phil enters carrying a suitcase. He looks at his watch. Pat enters with her bag at the moment Edna comes in to cross the foyer. There is a "moment"

Edna Well, you've got him you scheming bitch!
Phil Edna—just leave it out.
Edna You've been after him since you got here. I know all about you from your friends. You've only just buried one husband and you're after someone else's.
Phil Edna, this isn't helping.
Pat I don't want to have a row with you, Edna. What's happened has happened and there's nothing more to say. If you'd both been happily married it would have been different. But this is our chance for a bit of happiness.
Phil And we're taking it.
Edna (*on the verge of tears*) You never worked at this marriage.
Phil You don't work at a marriage—you work at a job.
Edna (*on the verge of tears*) I hope you both rot in hell!

Phil and Pat exit

The last few minutes of the play switch from the bus station and the bus speeding towards Sunderland, back to the hotel and the dance

Edna is on her own on stage

All the dancers enter and stand under the lights

The light as ever strikes the mirror ball and shatters into a thousand reflections

The bus station. Pat is sitting on her suitcase, her umbrella in her hand, Phil approaches through the dusk

Cut to the ballroom. Edna has just put a tape on, people are getting up to dance

Edna (*on mike*) Take your partners please for the veleta.

Music, shots of couples. Cut to the bus and people embarking. Pat and Phil taking their seats. Music over all this. Cut to Edna dancing with Jessie, the mirror ball turning becomes the headlights of the bus sweeping through the dark night across the moors. Interior of bus. Pat and Phil looking out at the darkness gathering across the moors

Pat She knows we're coming, our Kitty, she thinks it's dead funny.
Phil Are you happy, love?
Pat Ay, are you?
Phil Delirious, bloody delirious. We're going to enjoy ourselves, Pat. It's goin' to be all right.
Pat Ay, get supped up. Gi us a smile an' gerrum in.
Phil }
Pat } (*together*) You're a long time dead.

Cut to Edna on stage

Edna (*on mike*) Take your partners please for the last tango.

The music starts—"Jealousy". Edna walks across to Kathleen and they get up dancing, bust to bust

The dancers part to make a through-way as the backstage Lights reveal a sunset and Pat and Phil, leading the cast, dance into it

CURTAIN

FURNITURE AND PROPERTY LIST

ACT I

Scene 1

The coach

On stage: Two rows of seats on trolleys

Off stage: Suitcases **(Company)**
Crate of Guinness and light ale, carrier bag with 3 fezzes **(Jimmy)**

Personal: **Jimmy:** party hat

Scene 2

The hotel foyer

On stage: Reception desk

Scene 3

The amusement arcade

On stage: Space invaders
Fruit machines
Bingo
Dayglo panda
Lucky dip machine with spanner key-ring, ring in box

Scene 4

The jet shop

On stage: Counter with trays of jet jewellery, art deco badge

Personal: **Pat:** money

Scene 5

The Abbey

On stage: Bench

Off stage: Table **(Clare** and **Debbie)**

Scene 6

The hotel dining-room

On stage: Tables with used plates, cutlery, etc.
Chairs

Scene 7

The ballroom

On stage: Tables. *On them:* drinks
Chairs
Small stage. *On it:* tape recorder, microphone (practical)
Mirror ball

Scene 8

The beach

On stage: Rocks, pebbles, split pebbles, sea-wrack
Hammer for **Phil**

Scene 9

The ballroom

On stage: As Scene 7

Set: Cowboy hat on small stage for **Phil**
Raffle prizes on small stage

Scene 10

The pier

On stage: Railing

ACT II

Scene 1

The ballroom

On stage: As ACT I, Scene 7

Set: Small prizes, electric organ on small stage

Off stage: Wind-up gramophone with record, bones **(Henry)**
Dishcloth **(Debbie)**

Scene 2

The beach

On stage: As ACT I, Scene 8

Set: Dead seagull by rock pool

Last Tango in Whitby   41

                    SCENE 3

The ballroom
On stage: As ACT I, SCENE 7
Set: Prizes on small stage
Personal: **Pat:** handbag containing plastic dog turd

                    SCENE 4

The tearoom
On stage: Tables
             Chairs
Off stage: Counter with cups, saucers, etc., tea urn **(Tea Girls)**
Personal: **Kathleen:** handbag with hankie, money

                    SCENE 5

A shelter on the prom
On stage: Bench
Personal: **Pat:** hankie

                    SCENE 6

The foyer
On stage: Reception desk with tannoy (practical)
Personal: **Jimmy:** pipe, pouch of tobacco

                    SCENE 7

The foyer/ballroom/bus station
On stage: As before
Off stage: Suitcase **(Phil)**
             Bag, umbrella **(Pat)**
Personal: **Phil:** wrist-watch, tickets

LIGHTING PLOT

Property fittings required: mirror ball
Various simple interior and exterior settings

ACT I

To open; General lighting on coach

Cue 1	As different pieces of action happen on the coach *Lighting changes focus attention*	(Page 1)
Cue 2	As actors dance off coach *Crossfade to lighting on hotel foyer*	(Page 6)
Cue 3	As actors tango off on trip round town *Golden warm lighting*	(Page 7)
Cue 4	As women dance round to jet shop *Crossfade to jet shop*	(Page 8)
Cue 5	As women dance on *Crossfade to Abbey—back projection to suggest Abbey*	(Page 9)
Cue 6	As women dance off and waitresses dance on *Crossfade to dining-room*	(Page 9)
Cue 7	As **Clare** and **Debbie** dance off *Crossfade to ballroom—light on mirror ball first, then dancers*	(Page 11)
Cue 8	As waltz ends *Light on mirror ball as it spins, then hard fade to Black-out*	(Page 14)
Cue 9	As SCENE 8 opens *Grey light, back projection to suggest a sea horizon*	(Page 14)
Cue 10	As **Pat** and **Phil** dance off *Crossfade to ballroom*	(Page 16)
Cue 11	As dancers move upstage dancing *Lighting on forestage to suggest pier—shadow of ironwork, back projection of moon on sea*	(Page 17)

ACT II

To open: Lighting on ballroom

Cue 12	They laugh *Light on mirror ball as it spins for a few minutes*	(Page 22)
Cue 13	As **Debbie** and **Clare** waltz off *Crossfade to beach*	(Page 24)

Last Tango in Whitby

Cue 14	**Phil** and **Pat** waltz off slowly *Crossfade to ballroom*	(Page 26)
Cue 15	**Maureen** and **Jessie** dance off *Crossfade to tearoom—afternoon*	(Page 28)
Cue 16	**Kathleen**, **Jessie** and **Maureen** exit *Crossfade to shelter on prom—mellow light as sun sinks in west*	(Page 30)
Cue 17	**Kathleen**, **Maureen**, **Pat** and **Jessie** dance off *Crossfade to foyer*	(Page 32)
Cue 18	As dancers enter *Crossfade to ballroom; light on mirror ball; light on forestage as bus station*	(Page 38)
Cue 19	As dancers part *Sunset effect at back of stage*	(Page 38)

EFFECTS PLOT

ACT I

Cue 1	As SCENE 1 begins Music: "Last Tango" or "Summer Holiday"	(Page 1)
Cue 2	When actors are settled on coach Music: "Una Paloma Blanca"	(Page 1)
Cue 3	**Henry:** "We're here." Music: "Hernando's Hideaway"	(Page 6)
Cue 4	**Jimmy:** "... back for tea, right?" Music: "Mississippi Dip—Swanee"	(Page 7)
Cue 5	As actors tango off on trip round town Sound of seagulls, space invaders, fruit machines, bingo, music: "The Gay Gordons"	(Page 8)
Cue 6	**Pat:** "... bloody good time. Come on." Music: Military Two-step	(Page 8)
Cue 7	**Pat:** "... I'll pin it on now." They dance on Music: Military Two-step	(Page 9)
Cue 8	**Pat:** "... hungry watching 'em." Music: Military Two-step	(Page 9)
Cue 9	**Clare** and **Debbie** dance off Music: "Maybe It's Because I'm a Londoner"	(Page 11)
Cue 10	**Phil** switches on tape recorder Music: Tango	(Page 11)
Cue 11	As **Pat** and **Jessie** dance and others freeze Stop music	(Page 11)
Cue 12	**Jessie:** "Never mind love." Music for a short while, then stop	(Page 12)
Cue 13	**Phil:** "... all-time favourites The Slush." Music: "The Slush" and "Knock Three Times"	(Page 12)
Cue 14	**Phil:** "... sinks slowly in the bay." Hawaiian music	(Page 12)
Cue 15	After **Phil** and **Pat** have been dancing for a few minutes Stop music	(Page 13)
Cue 16	**Pat:** "... you do, don't you?" Music for a short while then stop	(Page 13)
Cue 17	**Kathleen:** "Act your age." Music for a short while then stop	(Page 13)

Last Tango in Whitby   45

Cue 18	**Pat:** "... very good listener." Music for a short while then stop	(Page 14)
Cue 19	As SCENE 8 opens Gulls calling, waves on beach—continue in background	(Page 14)
Cue 20	As **Pat** and **Phil** dance off Fade gull and sea noises, then bring up music for barn dance	(Page 16)
Cue 21	**Phil:** "... for the square tango." Music: "It's Now or Never"	(Page 16)
Cue 22	After **Phil** and **Pat** have been dancing for a few minutes Stop music	(Page 16)
Cue 23	**Pat:** "... I'll be there." Music for a short while then stop	(Page 16)
Cue 24	**Kathleen:** "... what's going on." Music for a short while then stop	(Page 16)
Cue 25	**Joan:** "I'm not so sure." Music for a short while then stop	(Page 17)
Cue 26	**Pat:** "... so sudden in a way." Music for a short while, then stop as dance ends	(Page 17)
Cue 27	**Edna:** "... for second and third." Music: Waltz in my Heart	(Page 17)
Cue 28	As dancers move upstage and off Fade music	(Page 17)
Cue 29	**Pat:** "... some bother you know." Music: "Falling in Love Again"	(Page 19)

ACT II

Cue 30	As SCENE 1 opens Music: Tango—fade as **Phil** speaks	(Page 20)
Cue 31	**Edna:** "... a bloody move on." Music jerks into life: Wilson, Kepple and Betty Sand Dance	(Page 20)
Cue 32	**Jimmy**, **Joan** and **Pat** exit Cut music	(Page 20)
Cue 33	**Phil:** "... Alice and Edie." Music as **Alice** and **Edie** perform their dance	(Page 20)
Cue 34	**Henry** plays gramophone Music: "William Tell Overture" or "Radetsky March" on gramophone, which keeps winding down, then speeding up as **Henry** winds it up, eventually with spring breaking and music going faster and faster, then stopping	(Page 21)
Cue 35	**Jessie** is ready to sing Music: "When You Were Sweet Sixteen" on organ	(Page 21)
Cue 36	**Edna:** "... the St Bernard's Waltz." Music: "St Bernard's Waltz"—softly	(Page 22)

Cue 37	**Jessie** and **Maureen** get up to dance *Increase music*	(Page 22)
Cue 38	As **Henry** and **Edna** dance downstage *Stop music*	(Page 22)
Cue 39	**Henry**: "I have done." *Music for a short while, then stop as* **Phil** *and* **Pat** *dance forward*	(Page 22)
Cue 40	**Pat** and **Phil** exit *Music*	(Page 23)
Cue 41	**Edna** switches off tape *Stop music*	(Page 23)
Cue 42	**Debbie:** "... Geriatric Gavotte." *Waltz music—fade as Scene 2 opens*	(Page 24)
Cue 43	**Pat:** "... a fossil all my life." *Music: "When I Grow Too Old to Dream"; gull calls*	(Page 26)
Cue 44	When **Phil** and **Pat** are ready for SCENE 3 *Fade music*	(Page 26)
Cue 45	**Pat:** "Come up and see me sometime." *Music: "March of the Mods"—fade when contestants are all lined up in front of stage*	(Page 26)
Cue 46	**Edna** turns on tape *Music: "Love Locked Out"*	(Page 27)
Cue 47	**Maureen** and **Jessie** dance off *Fade music*	(Page 28)
Cue 48	**Kathleen:** "Jessie, come on." *Music: "Boy Next Door"*	(Page 30)
Cue 49	As SCENE 5 opens *Fade music; bring up seagulls and waves*	(Page 30)
Cue 50	**Pat:** "You wicked old cow." *Music: Military Two-step—fade as Scene 6 opens*	(Page 32)
Cue 51	**Edna:** "... for the veleta." *Music: Veleta*	(Page 38)
Cue 52	**Edna:** "... for the last tango." *Music: "Jealousy"*	(Page 38)

MADE AND PRINTED IN GREAT BRITAIN BY
LATIMER TREND & COMPANY LTD PLYMOUTH
MADE IN ENGLAND